J 583.99 THO
Thomson, Ruth
A sunflower's life cycle

070610

Let's Look at Life Cycles

A Sunflower's Life Cycle

Ruth Thomson

PowerKiDS press

Published in 2010 by The Rosen Publishing Group Inc.
29 East 21st Street, New York, NY 10010

First Edition

Managing Editor: Victoria Brooker
Concept Designer: Paul Cherrill

Library of Congress Cataloging-in-Publication Data

Thomson, Ruth, 1949-
   A sunflower's life cycle / Ruth Thomson. -- 1st ed.
      p. cm. -- (Let's look at life cycles)
   Includes index.
   ISBN 978-1-61532-219-0 (library binding)
   ISBN 978-1-61532-230-5 (pbk.)
   ISBN 978-1-61532-231-2 (6-pack)
   1. Sunflowers--Juvenile literature. 2. Sunflowers--Life cycles--Juvenile literature. I. Title. II. Series: Let's look at life cycles.
   QK495.C74T47 2010
   583'.99--dc22
                                    2009024194

Photographs:
Cover, title page, 4, 5 Aflo/naturepl.com; 2, 13, 16 Nature Production/naturepl.com; 6 © James McQuillan/istockphoto.com; 6 (inset) Adam White/naturepl; 7 © Bobhdeering/Alamy; 8 © Nigel Cattlin/Alamy; 9 © Nigel Cattlin/Alamy; 10 © Elena Elisseeva/istockphoto.com; 11, 12, 17 Papilio; 14 © Matej Michelizza/istockphoto.com; 15 osf/photolibrary.com; 18 David Shale/naturepl; 19 © zoran simin/istockphoto.com; 20 Bildarchiv/Photolibrary.com; 21© Ron Watts/CORBIS

Manufactured in China

CPSIA Compliance Information: Batch #WAW0102PK: For Further Information

contact Rosen Publishing, New York, New York at 1-800-237-9932

Web Sites

Due to the changing nature of Internet links, PowerKids Press has developed an online list of Web sites related to the subject of this book. This site is updated regularly. Please use this link to access this list: http://www.powerkidslinks.com/lllc/flower/

Contents

What are sunflowers?

Sunflowers are tall flowering plants.
In the summer, their large flowers have
lots of bright yellow petals.

A sunflower
can grow as
tall as your
classroom.

4

Sunflowers always turn toward
the sun and follow it wherever
it is in the sky.

Planting seeds

Every sunflower starts as a seed.
The seed coat is hard and dry.
This protects the seed inside.

seed

seed coat

Sunflower seeds are good to eat.
Birds find the seeds tasty, too.

**Sunflower seeds
can be used to
make cooking oil
and margarine.**

Roots grow

In the spring, people plant the seeds in warm, damp soil. The hard seed coat splits. A root appears.

The root grows down into the soil.

Smaller roots sprout from the main root. The roots have tiny hairs. These take in water from the soil.

A sunflower seed needs water, air, and warmth to grow.

9

A shoot sprouts

A shoot grows upward. It breaks
through the soil into the open air.

seed coat

Two seed leaves open out.
These are small and plump.

These seed leaves contain food for the growing shoot.

Leaves appear

The shoot grows taller. New leaves appear.
These leaves use sunlight, water, and air
to make food.

Can you see
how the
leaves grow
in pairs?

stem

The plant grows taller. The stem
is thick and strong. More leaves sprout.
The roots grow longer and spread
out to hold the plant firmly
in the ground.

Flowers open

A flower bud grows at the top of the stem.
Green sepals protect the petals inside.
Slowly, the sepals unfold.

What can you
see under the
sepals?

petals

sepal

leaf

stem

The sunflower opens. Its flower head
is made up of hundreds of tiny flowers.
These are called florets.

Bees pollinate

The bright yellow petals attract bees.
They come to feed on nectar. As they crawl
over the florets, they become covered with pollen.

When the bees fly to other sunflowers, they brush some of the pollen onto other florets. This is called pollination.

Can you see how bees carry pollen?

Bees take pollen back to their nest as food.

Seeds grow

Once the florets are pollinated, the petals wilt and fall off. The leaves shrivel and turn brown. Tiny seeds begin to swell.

Soon, the flower head is full of seeds. The ripe seeds make the flower head so heavy that it droops over.

Each flower head can have up to 1,000 seeds.

From seed to sunflower

As the flower head dries, some seeds fall out. Birds come to feed on the seeds, but they often drop some.

These seeds may grow into
new sunflowers next spring.

Sunflower life cycle

In the spring, a seed is planted. First it grows a root, then a shoot. Soon leaves and a flower appear. After pollination, seeds begin to grow.

seeds
A seed is planted.

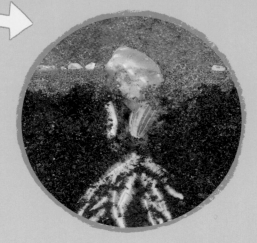

roots and shoot
Roots grow down in the ground then a shoot grows up.

flowers
The petals fall off and seeds grow.

flowers and leaves
Leaves grow and a flower bud and petals appear.

Make a paper plate sunflower

Make a colorful sunflower to brighten up a room.

You will need:

- paper plate
- yellow crepe paper
- green card
- scissors
- glue

1. Cut out lots of big petals from yellow crepe paper.

2. Cover a paper plate with glue. Stick down a ring of petals.

3. Overlap another ring of petals on top. Crumple the leftover scraps into balls. Glue them into a circle of florets in the center of the plate.

4. Roll green crepe paper into a stem. Tape it to the back of the plate.

5. You could make several sunflowers to give to your friends.

Glossary and Further Information

bud the top of a shoot that will open and grow into a leaf or flower

floret a tiny flower in a flower head

flower head a flower made up of lots of tiny florets

nectar the sweet liquid inside a flower that attract insects

pollen the yellow grains of powder inside a flower

root the part of a plant that grows down into the ground and takes in water

sepals the green flaps that protect a flower bud

shrivel to dry up and die

stem the stalk of a plant. Leaves and flowers grow on the stem.

Books

Life Cycle of a Sunflower
by Angela Royston
(Heinemann Library, 2009)

The Life of a Sunflower
by Clare Hibbert
(Raintree Publishers, 2004)

The Life Cycle of a Sunflower
by Linda Tagliaferro
(Capstone Press, 2007)

Index